LIBERTY

Enlightening the World

LIBERTY
Enlightening the World

Poem & Artwork

Vijali Hamilton

WORLD WHEEL PRESS
Santa Fe, New Mexico 87505
USA

© 2005-2021 Vijali Hamilton. All Rights Reserved.

No part of this book may be reproduced, stored in a retrieval system, or transmitted by any means without the written permission of the author.

First published 2006

Revised edition published 2021

Library of Congress Control Number: 2005907026

ISBN: 978-0-9789055-3-8

Printed in the United States of America

To order books contact World Wheel Press.

WORLD WHEEL PRESS
662 Alta Vista St. Suite D18
Santa Fe, New Mexico 87505
USA

www.WorldWheel.org

info@WorldWheel.org

DEDICATED

to our original American dream

PRELUDE

Liberty Enlightening the World is a hymn to the Statue of Liberty, a cry for survival, a longing for living the oldest, purest, implicit ideals of humanity. Now in this age of America's conflictive power and influence, may this evocation, inspired by India's ancient prayers to the Goddess, augment the growing global voice of liberty. To my joy when doing research on the Statue of Liberty, I found that her correct and original name to be "Liberty Enlightening the World." Creating this book is my prayer for global peace in the face of the challenges of the twenty first century.

Vijali

Give me your tired, your poor,
Your huddled masses yearning to breathe free,
The wretched refuse of your teeming shore.
Send these, the homeless, tempest-tossed to me,
I lift my lamp beside the golden door!

> Fragment of the inscription on the base of the Statue of Liberty, from a poem by Emma Lazarus

Liberty, rise like the sun....

LIBERTY
Enlightening the World

O Liberty!
  with all our hearts we contemplate Your form;
Your beautiful face with noble brow,
  Your full breasts and tall stature
    revealed by Your graceful flowing robe.
Rise like the sun, holding in Your right hand
  the light of the world.
O Woman! How can we describe
  Your thought-transcending form.
You who exists in the hearts of all beings,
  who are giver of liberation.
O Liberty Enlightening the World! Salutations to You.

O Mighty Woman!
Your beacon-hand rising high into the sky,
    welcomes the weary, the poor, the homeless.
Giver of refuge, Your left hand supports
    the declaration of our independence,
    our right to breathe free, to walk proudly.
At Your sandaled feet, Your broken shackle lies as
    victory over the tyranny of the elite.
O Mother of Exiles! Remover of our poverty and pain,
    all reverence to You.

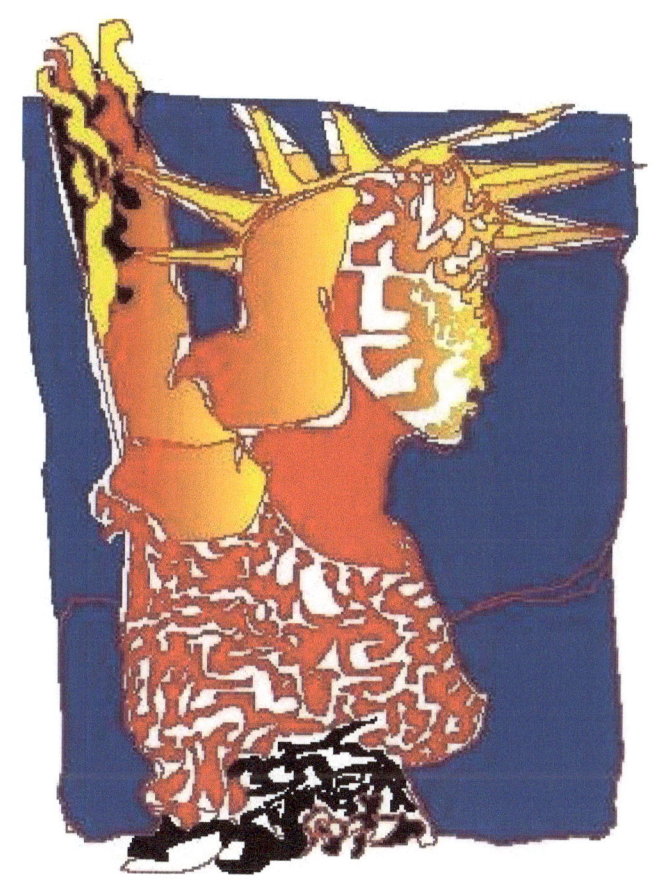

O Liberty, You are fire

O Liberty!

We contemplate Your form: our guide holding torch,
     who is light Herself.

Standing on an island of earth,
     You are earth, creatrix of the world
     full of sounds and their meaning.

Surrounded by water, as liquid drapery,
     You are water, thirst quencher of the world.

Holding fire in your hand, You are fire,
     destroyer of the darkness of ignorance.

Standing in space,
     You are our inner space.

Cloaked in air,
     Your lips are air, breath of the world.

Liberty! We salute You.

Holding fire, You are fire

Rising from Your ocean of compassion

O Joyous One! Queen of America.
You are always with beaming face.
We shall never forget You,
    who are the giver of happiness.
O Woman, how can the ignorant,
    whose minds are restless with doubt and dispute,
Know Your form, exquisite with the mist of sea,
    rising from Your ocean of compassion.
Proud Lady! You are beautiful.

O Formidable One!
    whose greatly abounding strength
    destroys the darkness of our illusions.
O Liberty! we take refuge with You.
O Eternal One! Men and women worship You
    under various names:
You are the Primordial One,
    Mother of wolf and lion, hawk and fish,
    the countless creatures on this earth,
Therefore we worship Your breasts, Mother of all.
Origin of the world You are,
    yet you have no origin.
How few know Your nature, or Your inner reality.
You are the atom and the ever-pervading.
You are the substance of the universe;
    You it is who exists within all forms of life.
You exist in Your fullness everywhere,
    within everything undivided.
We take refuge in Your sacred name,
    "Liberty Om,"
    springing from the beginnings of time.
You, the Spouse of the Infinite! salutations to You.

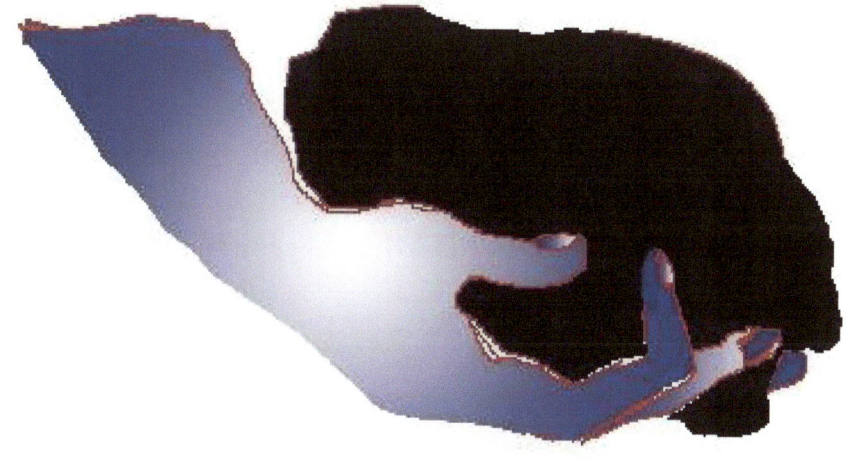

Remover of Darkness

O Spouse of the Eternal!
We adore You, whose body shines
    splendor of a thousand rising suns,
    holding with one hand Your flame,
You are beautiful with form, amorous, charming.
O Liberty! You are united with Your mate the Infinite.
We worship in our hearts, O Liberty,
    Your body moist with nectar from that union,
Beautiful as the splendor of lightning,
You whose body is intelligence itself,
    whose substance is existence.
Having taken refuge with You,
    we shall never in our hearts forget You.
O Abode of Bliss, who gives birth to prosperity,
    we salute You.

O Liberator!
May Your glory be forever in our hearts,
Whose substance is pure knowledge and bliss.
With the rays from Your crown,
    dispel the darkness which covers our hearts.
Burn, burn our limitations
    and grant us our full inheritance.
You are Knowledge itself.
You are beyond the reach of the scriptures;
    they sing of You but do not know You.
May we know You.
O Giver of Liberation!
    whose power is beyond all understanding,
    grant to us this favor.

It is You who grant success to the tongue and all forms of knowledge

O Liberty! even an ignorant man or woman,
    meditating on Your form,
    acquires all poetic power,
    for You are the presiding deity of speech.
Burn, burn, dispel the darkness of our thoughts.
It is You who grant success to the tongue
    in the attainment of all forms of knowledge.
We pray to You, come to our tongues and never leave us.
Take our confusion away, help our intelligence stay,
May we be free from sorrow.
In time of peril may we never be bewildered;
May our minds flow freely without impediment.
Those who take shelter with You need fear no danger,
    since they become a refuge to themselves.
O Mother, who has shown Thyself in many forms:
    in the sciences,
For the maintenance of the world in agriculture
    and trade,
And in the great arts: sculpture, music, painting,
    literature, dance, drama—You illumine us.
Through Your light of knowledge,
    You are the supreme destroyer of our pain.
O Liberty! be gracious to us, who else is there but You?

Those who worship power, create separation by its nature

Alas! We are unhappy people,
    who when the Space Age,
    the complexity of ages, has come,
    do not worship You.
Instead, people cunning and skilled
    in the scriptures and politics
    have made us devoted
    to the worship of greed and war.
Those who worship power with devotion,
    create separation by its nature,
    taking away from the poor,
    adding wealth to the rich.
Protectress of the lowly and those in need,
    we worship You with our tears.

Battlefield of our minds

O Destroyer of our Illusion!
      You could kill upon the battlefield of our minds
The enemies grown strong and tall within us,
      taking shape as fame and power.
The field of battle would seem to have been swept
      by a tempest,
Most hideous it would be,
      thickly spread with the limbs of greed
      and dead bodies of guilt
in whose blood and flesh birds of prey quench
      their thirst and appease their hunger.

You are light itself—protect us

O Queen of the Universe! and its guardian,
    who takes away the addictions of mind,
Alleviate our drowning, alas!
    as we are in the endless ocean of illusion,
    forgetting our real nature.
You are light itself;
    protect us from our shortsightedness,
    the genocide of our indigenous peoples,
    the assault and murder of our children.
Make cease at once this confusion of the whole world:
    feeling that war will bring peace and safety,
    and the great danger of nuclear war,
    our own self destruction,
    and the raping of our earth
    by destroying our forests,
    poisoning our waters,
    polluting our air.
O Mother Liberty! protect our home,
    this world; we are Your children.

You have made your abode in our hearts

O Liberty! our Supreme Lady!
    be gracious for the sake of the world.
O Bestower of Generosity of Spirit!
Devoid of attachment are You,
    who has made Your abode in our hearts
    and in the hearts of those
    whom we think of as enemies.
O Mother of all!! You give life to all things,
    since as they are parts of You.
Reverence to You, who dwells in all lands,
O Liberty!
Let us meditate upon this light held in Your hand.
Our salutations to You!!

Let us meditate upon this light held in Your hand

BIOGRAPHY

Beginning in 1986, when she became inspired by a dream and was prompted to embark upon a quest for global peace, artist, writer and filmmaker Vijali Hamilton traveled from one country to another, leaving behind magnificent environmental stone sculptures as a gift to the communities in which she lived. Her journey ranged from India, Tibet, China, Siberia, Japan and the Middle East to Senegal, Native North America, and the Andes and Amazonian region of Ecuador. Vijali named this initiative, *World Wheel, Global Peace Through the Arts* (www.WorldWheel.org).

In each locale, she developed community-based performance ceremonies in which are heard the voices of traditional peoples rising clear and strong. Vijali's collaborative, creative approach in each community made these artful and spiritual events into expressive forums for voicing their residents' hopes and fears.

Vijali continues to address the concerns of our times through this small but powerful book. *Liberty Enlightening the World* calls for the world to join hands as one earthly family and to walk lightly on our planet while in harmony with Nature and one another.

Vijali's other books include, *World Wheel: One Woman's Quest for Global Peace; Of Earth and Fire;* and, *Listening to Stone: Awakening to the Spiritual in the Natural World.* Her feature length films include: *Wheel of the World, One Woman's Creative Journey for Global Peace.*

Poem composed on Boney Mountain, California, May 1, 1983.

Artworks, book design and cover created 2001 by Vijali Hamilton.

www.ingramcontent.com/pod-product-compliance
Lightning Source LLC
Chambersburg PA
CBHW042125040426
42450CB00002B/71